Stone House

Legends &

Lore

By

Marci Lynn McGuinness

Copyright © April 1998
Second Printing, 2008

ISBN: 978-0-938833-28-4

Published in conjunction with   Stone House, Inc.

Shore Publications, P. O. Box 26, Chalk Hill, PA 15421
www.ohiopyle.info or www.shorepublications.info
shorepublications@yahoo.com

FORWARD

Dear Readers,

The Stone House that Andrew Stewart built on the great National Road in Chalk Hill, Pennsylvania has served travelers and locals since 1822. Its walls and grounds hold a history that takes you through the hey days of the Old Pike when the National Road (Route 40) was the gateway to the west. A Confederate soldier is said to have appeared here from Civil War days. Coal Barons and Steel Magnates joined Mr. George Titlow through a time of wealth and entertainment during the coal and coke boom of southwestern Pennsylvania.

We'll see what happened when Mr. Titlow passed away after owning the Stone House for 31 years. Fannie Ross will tell us of her move to the mountains in the 1960's as the little Italian woman with the terrific sauce.

You'll hear from those who worked and lived in a building that reeks of heritage and sometimes, mystery. Was there a murder way back when?

New owners share their first two years in business in the Historic Stone House. Remodeling, Steeler Nights, Radio Days, and Special Event photographs depict a new era of memorable dinners and, if Millie is your waitress, many laughs.

I give you Stone House Legends & Lore.

Marci Lynn McGuinness
Author & Stone House Fan

Contents

The Fayette
Springs Hotel

Andrew Stewart opened the Fayette Springs Hotel resort in
1822 for National Road travelers.

Andrew Stewart

Biography of a Mountain Boy

Andrew Stewart began his life like many Fayette Countians. He was born on a farm on June 11, 1791 in McClellandtown, Pennsylvania where his father served as Justice of the Peace. His parents, Abraham (from York) and Mary Oliphant Stewart (of Chester County), traded this property to William McLelland for a Wharton Township farm called "The Land of Cakes".

The eldest of six children, Andrew worked the Gibbon Glade land and attended school until he was eighteen years old. The young man proceeded to both teach school and clerk at an iron furnace while saving his hard earned funds. The ambitious Andrew put himself through Washington College, returned to Uniontown to read law and was accepted into the Fayette County Bar on January 9, 1815. This same year, at 24, he was elected to the Pennsylvania legislature and then re-elected for a three year term.

At this point he decided to run for the State Senate, but President Polk, realizing Stewart's great potential, appointed him District Attorney. In 1820 he resigned this office to take his place in the United States Congress where he represented our district as a member of the 17th, 20th, 22nd, 23rd, 26th, 27th, 28th, 29th, and 30th Congresses.

In Congress, Stewart's contemporaries were John Q. Adams, Abraham Lincoln, Andrew Jackson, Martin Van Buren, Andrew Johnson, John Tyler, Millard Fillmore, Franklin Pierce, and James Buchanan.

Stewart, always inventive, distributed free watermelons during the campaign in 1822. He won his seat in Congress by a wide margin, defeating Mr. Clevenger of Greene County. During his political career Andrew Stewart became a land baron, amassing 80,000 acres throughout Fayette County!

The Fayette County Bar Association Circa 1909

Andrew Stewart earned his way into the Fayette County Bar Association at 24 years of age in 1815. Here, in 1909, George Titlow stands to the right on the front porch steps as he hosts a meeting for the twentieth century bar. Titlow soon built a vast addition to the old Fayette Springs Hotel and named it his Stone House.

As Stewart became successful, he invested his money in properties and businesses. At the height of his career he owned over 80,000 acres of Fayette County. Two of his first purchases were the lands where he built his two Fayette Springs Hotels in Chalk Hill. The first sat just south of the National Road on Fayette Springs Road. He built a hotel and cabins here . There was a sulphur spring across the road that attracted travelers from across the country. As business grew and the National Road became the gateway to the west, Stewart commissioned Colonel Cuthbert Wiggins to construct a resort along the Pike nearby.

The new Fayette Springs Hotel opened in 1822, affording spring dwellers a comfortable inn. Billiards, a ten-pin alley, swings, fine meals, and overnight accommodations attracted wealthy visitors. The springs fell into disrepair but can be located today on the little creek.

The Fayette Springs were believed to have curative powers!

The Distinguished
Andrew Stewart
1791 - 1872

While running his hotels and representing our area in the United States Congress, Stewart built a block of brick buildings along Morgantown and Main Streets in Uniontown, Pennsylvania and called it, Stewart's Row. He lived here, ran his law practice, and leased to shopkeepers and doctors. Soon he built the Clinton House on Main Street next to the old court house and made his home there. Then built a mansion on the east side of town and leased the Clinton House for a hotel.

The long time Congressman became known across the country as "Tariff Andy". He led the fight for tariffs and was a great spokesman for the National Road, Chesepeake & Ohio Canal, and later, the Baltimore and Ohio Railroad. He was a member of the Democratic party until 1828 when their stand on the tariff led him to the Whig party. He helped found the Republican party! Our Andy believed that American industries should be developed and fostered by applying tariffs. Here is his policy in his words, "Protect and cherish your national industry by a wise system of finance, selecting in the first place those articles which you can and ought to supply to the extent of your own wants-food, clothing, habitation, and defense-and to these give ample and adequate protection, so as to secure at all times an abundant supply at home. Next select the luxuries consumed by the rich and impose on them such duties that the wants of the government may require for revenue, and then take the necessaries of life consumed by the poor, and articles which we can not supply, used in manufactories, and make them free, or subject to the lowest rate of duty."

Tariff Andy was idolized by voters. He owned the Madison College in Uniontown when during the Civil War it was turned into a Soldier's Orphans Home. He gave $10,000.00 to hard working graduate students each year until the day he died.

With all his duties and business ventures, Stewart found time for love. He married Elizabeth Shriver of Cumberland, Maryland in 1825 and they had six children. Her father was David Shriver, Superintendent of the Eastern Division of the National Road from Cumberland to Brownsville. The following are their children's names and dates of death: Fannie, 1836; Lt. William, January 24, 1870; Elizabeth, May 4, 1894; David Shriver (the eldest), August 21, 1897;

Col. Andrew, October 19, 1903; and Albert, November 25, 1916. Lt.-Commander William F. Stewart lost his life when the British steamer hit the U.S. Oneida in the waters off the coast of Yokohama, Japan. His last words were, "No, let others take the boat. My duty is on board my ship."

Congressman Stewart built the Wharton Furnace in 1839. Canon balls were made here during the Civil War. The furnace ran through 1873 and was the major industry in Wharton Township during that time. Throughout his life he built eleven saw mills, four grist mills, many planing mills, a glass factory, four hotels, and rented over two hundred businesses and homes.

In 1848 he was nominated for the Vice Presidency of the United States of America by the Whig party at a Philadelphia convention. During the first round he won fourteen of the twenty two votes needed. The second round voted him in unanimously. For some unknown reason, the delegation chairman ran to the floor and prematurely announced that they could not decide upon a man. Filmore was subsequently nominated and confirmed before the mistake was brought to light. In 1849 President Zachary Taylor visited Uniontown with his family and distinguished gentlemen. They were traveling to Washington where he would take his Presidential seat. He spoke and stayed at the Clinton House. Taylor offered Stewrat the seat of Secretary of the Treasury but Stewart declined. When Taylor passed away Filmore became President, a position that rightly belonged to Stewart. In1850 Tariff Andy retired from public office to pursue his business interests.

At this time Stewart invested substantially in acreage surrounding the Ohiopyle Falls. He was the first to successfully harness the water power there running a thriving saw mill from above the drop.It was run by three Rainey turbine wheels giving it the power of one hundred and thirty horses. His youngest son, Albert managed this and the planing mill which was added in 1865. Many men found work here and the town prospered. The Stewarts proceeded to build homes for workers and sell lots to those who wanted to settle and work in the new Falls City. Stewart was a famous man of strong character and mind. He developed a wilderness along the Youghiogheny and led the fight to bring the Baltimore & Ohio Railroad here. Throughout his life he continued to be involved in all the important topics of the day through letters and speaking. He was a major player in the running of our country until his death in 1872.

Sons Andrew, Albert, and David worked with their father to run the vast business empire. They built a covered bridge over the Youghiogheny in 1850 and a wooden one over Meadow Run in 1871.While Falls City was constructed, a resort community was being surveyed for the Ferncliff Peninsula. Their father knew one day passenger trains would bring travelers to their paradise and money was to be made. He did not however, forsee the coal and coke boom, which meant his family would become more wealthy than even he had imagined.

In 1868 the first track was laid in the Falls City area. In 1870 the first train came through. In 1871 they redid a huge barn into the Ohiopyle Hotel and the first tourist boom of Ohiopyle began. Because Falls City was one of two cities with that name along the B&O, Stewart's Falls City was named Ohiopyle officially in 1891 when the town was incorporated into a borough. The name had been used through the years by Indians. It means white frothy water and/or beautiful falls. A very fitting image

Andrew Stewart passed away on July 16, 1872 at his home in Uniontown at eighty two years, one year after he succeeded in bringing the great railroad through his Youghiogheny paradise.

In 1877 Mrs. Elizabeth Stewart sold the Fayette Springs Hotel on the National Road to Captain John Messmore. By 1879 the Stewarts opened the posh Ferncliff Hotel in Ohiopyle. Although they had planned on building an entire town on the peninsula, the coal and coke boom kept them busy with their saw mills and hotels and saved the Ferncliff from further development. Outdoor hot tubs were built on the grounds with coal heated water. Wooden steps took you down to the falls from the hotel. A wooden boardwalk welcomed visitors from the railroad station to the hotel or down to the river where a band stand, pavillion, and bowling alley was set up. Nightly entertainment amused visitors who traveled round trip from Cumberland or Pittsburgh for one dollar.

The following men were pallbearers at Andrew Stewart"s funeral in 1872. They all belonged to the Fayette County Bar Association he was so involved in: W.H. Playford, G.W.K. Minor, William Baity, James Darby, Thomas B. Searight, A.D. Boyd, John D. Roddy, and Alfred Howell.

You will notice a Boyd in the following photograph with his son a score of years later:

The Ohiopyle House, 1892

Twenty years after Andrew Stewart's death, Civil War veterans gathered at his Ohiopyle House. His son, Colonel Andrew Stewart is among the men. Left to right: Oliver Sproul, Sr., William P. Jackson, J.T. Lambie, Arch Boyd, Deacon Morris, Squire Collins, Andy Hall, Frank Cunningham, John Williams, ---Smalley, unknown, unknown, Col. Andrew Stewart (facing right), unknown, Doc Shipley, Billy Williams, Alan Bryner (cane), George Potter, Rube Leonard, and Paul Stull.

Ferncliff Hotel

Seven years after Andrew Stewart's death, his family built the stylish Ferncliff Hotel and sold the Fayette Springs Hotel. It had four floors of luxury rooms, 800 electric lights and gas heat. Outdoor hot tubs soothed traveler's as they sipped cocktails and watched the Ohiopyle Falls flow.. The Ferncliff sat proudly on the knob of the Ferncliff Peninsula. This and a few cabins are the only buildings which were ever constructed here. During the 1930's and forties the Ferncliff fell to disrepair.

In 1958 Edgar Kaufmann gave this land to the Western Pennsylvania Conservancy. It is now part of Ohiopyle State Park.

Falls City , PA
Saw and Planing Mill
1897

 Andrew Stewart's sons built this enormous mill at the Ohiopyle Falls in 1879 when they opened the Ferncliff Hotel. They had smaller buildings here earlier. The mill was the center of productivity selling much of the lumber to mines during the great coal and coke boom. After the depression the Stewart family sold their land here and moved on.

Falls City 1897

Twenty five years after Andrew Stewart passed away, his dream lived on. Ohiopyle's Baltimore & Ohio Station bustles here. The Ferncliff archway shown on the right took visitors to the grand hotel via boardwalk. Notice the covered bridge in the background. The Ohiopyle House Hotel sat to the left of the train.

Stewart Mysteries

When researching history, you always have unanswered questions. There is no way of knowing some things. You can get a feel for the way you believe they must have been, but hunches are not proof in our world.

From my studies I know that a man named John Stewart was the first settler here in the Ohiopyle area. He was here as early as 1772 and raised an orchard. He was buried here around 1800 and his family left the area.

Another Stewart named Andrew (not OUR Andrew) lived on the same property on Kentuck Mountain as John after the others left. This leads me to believe they were very possibly related.

William Stewart settled Stewart's Landing (Connellsville) in 1753. His home was one that the Indians burned along with the Ohio Company's building then.

OUR Andrew Stewart had sons named Andrew and William. I believe pioneers John and William were OUR Andrew's elders. I have no proof and thus far no real family members have come forward with documentation.

A George Stewart used to own the property where Kentuck Knob is. A nice lady who is related to this man says they are not family of OUR Andrew Stewart. My gut tells me that somewhere along the family tree there are branches for all the Stewarts who settled this area. She says there are so many Stewarts in Scotland there could be many families here. On the same mountain, though? Maybe.

Another mystery, is why did the Stewart sons not develop Ferncliff Penninsula as planned?

The main mystery to me is this. I have been researching the Stewarts and Ohiopyle for seven years and want to know, Where are the Stewarts now?

Ferncliff

A Subdivision That Never Happened

In 1868, just four years before his death, Andrew Stewart had his youngest son Albert draw up plans to develop Ferncliff Peninsula into a resort town. Thborough we know as Ohiopyle is seen at bottom center of the survey. Across the river, the peninsula was laid out with over 300 building lots in addition to the grand hotel and grounds.

They donned the Ohiopyle Falls a great water power and watering place!

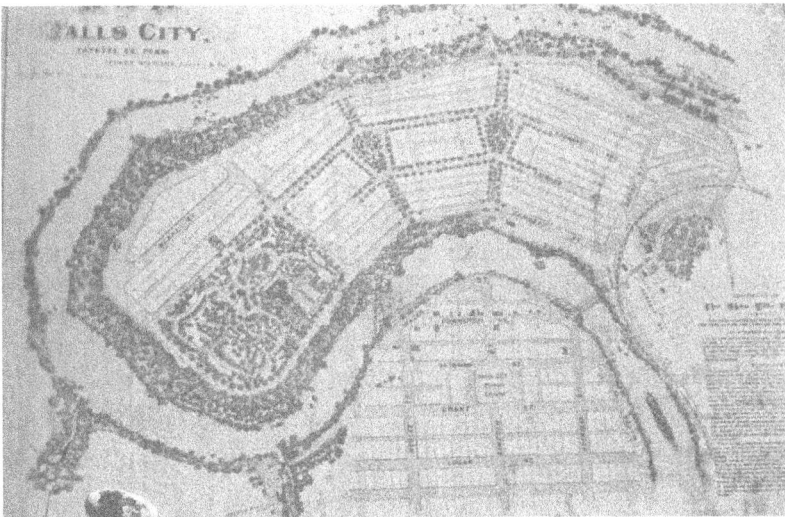

A Fayette Springs Mystery

I have searched high and low for a photograph of the first Fayette Springs Hotel on Fayette Springs Road. We know it burnt in 1879. Many have promised they had a picture somewhere, but I have yet to see one.

This makes the place mysterious to me. What did it look like? Was it wooden? Stone?

And what were those curative powers the spring had that drew so many from so far away? Did the sulphur water really heal people or just make them feel better like all cool streams?

The following is the contents of an advertisement from the Uniontown Genius of Liberty on May 13, 1852. (Contributed by Mark Miner of Wexford):

Fayette Springs

"This highly attractive and fashionable watering place has been leased, together with the Fayette Springs Hotel, adjacent thereto by the proprietor of the Farmington hotel on the National Road, who has secured the best cook and the best supplies of every kind, with a determination to please all his visitors. A new building with forty rooms has recently been added to the establishment. These Springs are surrounded by the most delightful and romantic

Mountain Scenery

in a cool climate, with pure air and pure water-true elements of health and God's greatest blessing to man on earth. The curative and purifying properties of these waters have been fully established by the fact that they have never failed to cure the worst cases of scrofula, the most inveternie sores, and other diseases of the blood, by drinking the water freely, and in case of eruptions, bathing and applying the stream externally.The waters are thoroughly chalybeate with portions of magnesia, salts, & e.

Besides, the Springs are located in the midst of classic ground, within an hours ride of

Washington's First Battle Field

at "Fort Necessity," where the entrenchments are still distinctly visible. General Braddock's and Jumonville's Graves, Dunbar's Encampment, Washington's Spring and Meadow, which he owned till he died. In the immediate vicinity are also several remarkable cultural curiosities, among those

Delaney's Cave

which may be explored for miles under the mountains; the

Celebrated Ohio Pile Falls

on the Youghiogheny River; the CUCUMBER CATARACT, descending from a shelving rock more than forty feet perpendicular. Game and Trout Fishing abound in the neighborhood. Saddles are furnished to visitors.

Visitors can pass from Brownsville daily in a drive of four or five hours to the Springs, over an excellent McAdamized road, about half the distance through one of the richest and most delightful agricultural regions in the country to Uniontown, and then eight miles further over the Laurel Mountain, presenting from its slopes and summit splendid views of the great western valley, with its rich, and beautiful scenery. In short, it is confidently believed that there is no watering place in the country, presenting stronger attractions to those seeking

Healthier Pleasure

than the "Fayette Springs;" and the undersigned is very certain they can nowhere find a greater disposition as these on more accommodating terms."

SEBASTIAN RUSH

Captain John Messmore & Others 1877 - 1909

On December 26, 1877 Mrs. Andrew (Elizabeth) Stewart sold the Fayette Springs Hotel along the National Road. The Old Pike had died down and the railroad took passengers and products where they needed to go. She then built the Ferncliff Hotel with her sons and enjoyed the Youghiogheny River in Ohiopyle.

Below: An 1897 Youghiogheny River Scene just below the Western Maryland Railroad Bridge above the falls. Any Stewarts in this crowd? Probably.

Captain John Messmore owned a restaurant and tavern in Uniontown when he bought the popular Fayette Springs Hotel from Elizabeth Stewart. He leased the business out to Samuel Lewis and then William Snyder. Hard times ensued on the National Road as the Railroad took over. The folk who had money traveled by train instead of coach, and cars were no around yet.

Although it was the onset of the coal and coke boom, there was no train depot in Farmington. Messmore's family sold part of the 440 acre parcel when he died in 1984. The next year Daniel Gibson of Uniontown sold 340 acres to Calvin L. Dean of Wharton Township for $6,000.00.

William H. Playford bought 98 acres here from Thomas McCollough in 1895 for $2,000.00.

On September 23, 1899 Sheriff George A. McCormick, High Sheriff of Fayette County, sold 98 acres plus 6 3/4 perches to A.D. Boyd for $4,700.00.

While Calvin Dean owned the Fayette Springs Hotel a William Darlington ran the business in 1892.

George Flavius Titlow & the Stone House 1909 - 1944

George Flavius Titlow
1864 - 1940

The above photograph was taken from a charcoal portrait found by Fannie Ross in the Stone House attic. We think it is from around 1910 - 1920.

On August 3, 1909, George Flavius Titlow of Uniontown, Pennsylvania, purchased the Fayette Springs Hotel on Farmington's National Road. He bought the building and 98 acres from Albert and Annie Boyd for $12,000.

When the papers were signed Titlow immediately hired carpenters and stone masons. They constructed an enormous addition to the structure of the Titlow family's new summer/weekend home. George Titlow named his mansion the Stone House and this name has held most of the days since.

The photograph below shows the newly remodeled Stone house along the dirt pike. In front of the three cars parked in the background is a man driving cattle. To the left behind the stone wall is a large table set up for a reunion. Circa 1920.

Titlow's Stone House, 1920

George Flavius Titlow was born in Uniontown, Pennsylvania on January 31, 1864. His father, Flavius B. Titlo (George added the "W" to the name Titlo) came from Middletown, Maryland where he had been raised in an historic Old Pike tavern. He was a tailor by trade but opened a general store in Uniontown and married Drusilla A. Beeson, daughter of Henry Beeson. George had four siblings; Henry, Elizabeth, and Annie who were his elders, and a younger brother named Walter Edward.

George went to public school until he was eighteen. He then worked in general merchandise with his father for four years after graduation. From 1886 - 1888 he was employed as a clerk at the Yough House in Connellsville, Pennsylvania. Soon he took over the management of the Hotel Marietta in Connellsville for seven years. During this time Rockwell and Marcus Marietta, in addition to owning the Hotel Marietta, organized both the Pittsburgh and Connellsville Brewing Companies. These were eventually, along with several smaller breweries, consolidated into the Pittsburgh Brewing Company which still thrives today.

On June 12, 1889 he married Anna M. Burus of Wilmington, Delaware and hence began his family of seven children. The year after his marriage he bought the Jennings House(West End Hotel) in Uniontown for $40,000.00. At the time this was the largest sum ever paid for a hotel in the county seat. Soon he purchased the McClelland House and remodeled it, selling it for $90,000.00 in 1903.

He then rested for two years. I use the term rested loosely here because, according to reports from those who knew him, George never rested. He was flambouyant and had enormous energy. My feeling for the man after doing so much research tells me he was very aware of the coal and coke boom happening around him, having a hand in a variety of businesses. He was elected to the town council from the First ward in 1900.

George bought the Frost House in 1905 and acquired the first hotel license for the place. He renamed it the Hotel Titlow. Coal Barons were solicited to invest in Titlow's plan for the most luxurious hotel the area has ever had. He bought the Lingo Block which was next to the Frost House on the west side. By 1906 he had a hotel standing four floors and extending back to Peter Street. This establishment of marble floors and walls and brass trimmings quickly became the headquarters for our country's most powerful coal, coke, and steel men. On May 16, 1906 a grand opening reception was held where over 1200 guests attended! The following is an excerpt from the Daily Standard of May 24, 1906:

"An opening for which beauty and elaborateness of appointments and general magnificence has probably never been equaled in Fayette County was that of the Hotel Titlow on Wednesday evening May 16, 1906 from 5 to 11 o'clock. Between 1200 and 1500 persons prominent and representative of the social, representative, and business life of the community, were present and joined in making it the greatest success of the kind ever recorded in Western Pennsylvania. Mr. Titlow was in his happiest mood and stood on his feet for seven hours and welcomed the guests, but was just as fresh and lively at the close as at the beginning. All of the receiving party were gracious and cordial and Mr. Titlow himself took just pride in what he had to offer his guests.On the other hand guests were pleased beyond measure and congratulated Mr. Titlow on his remarkable achievement in putting Uniontown on a par with large cities in the matter of an incredible hotel building.And the general expression was that it was only a man of consummate energy and enterprise and perseverance of Mr. Titlow who could make such a structure possible and feasible in Uniontown.The Hotel Titlow is the highest priced furnished hotel in Western Pennsylvania and is the only hotel run on the European Plan in Fayette County. Mr. Titlow has spared no trouble or expense in making it the very best hostelry of its size to be found anywhere. It is four stories in height and was improved at a cost of $100,000.00 for the real estate and hotel and $40,000.00 for the furnishings. All the furniture in the office and on the fourth floor is of mahogany and that on the other floors of quartered oak.

"Hard wood maple is used as flooring in the three upper stories, while the office is all in marble. There are 110 rooms in the hotel, of which 66 are bedrooms.

"The decorations for the opening were by the Baron Floral Company and the electric lights by Weller & Grey. Music was furnished by the West End Theatre Orchestra consisting of Ralph Dalton, violin; George W. Pooler of Greensburg, piano; Chas. B. Price, coronet; Luigi Barbiere, clarinet; and Procto McWilliams of Greensburg, drums."

You must keep in mind that this was during a great economical time in the county's history. Money flowed freely as coal barons became millionaires and the Hotel Titlow was home to hundreds of meetings held by the most powerful men of that time.

The hotel plans were drawn by architect Andrew B. Cooper and the renovations took almost a year to complete. The fire escape was built by Taylor & Dean and was tested by putting 30 large men on it. John D. Carr of Uniontown with a force of 16 men did the extensive marble and tile work. In the lobby is a Rutland Marble floor. Altman and 10 men did all the painting and Matt Allen and 6 artists handled decorating. William R. Miller supervised his staff of plumbers to complete the largest contract of its kind in the Uniontown area's history, except for the First National Bank. F.T. Evans and his men did the steam heating work and William Helmey manned a crew to run the electric wiring and long distance phones in each room. George supervised all the work himself, assisted by Samuel Daniels."

The hotel had its own ice plant, cold storage rooms, and fire company employing 8 men. There were 5 fire plugs in the building and a standpipe in the center of the hotel. Titlow also housed a distillery there. According to an ad in a 1912 Old Home Week program, they sold gallons of pure rye whiskey "Leading Brand Uniontown Special" for $2.00 to $4.00.

In addition to the main dining room there was a private dining room upstairs. The office had a large fireplace and a revolving door-the only one in the county. To have a revolving door on your office is a sure sign of huge amounts of business being negotiated!

George chose the best materials and craftsmen to build his hotel. When they opened the rooms were rented for $1.00 - 5.00 per day and meals began at 50 cents. Dick Rush ran the Titlow Hotel office.

Titlow Buys the Fayette Springs Hotel

George did well and in 1909 he bought the Fayette Springs Hotel in Farmington from Albert Boyd for $12,000.00. He employed many of the same craftsmen adding a huge addition to the front of the building. He put in parque floors and fancy woodwork with fireplaces in every room.

The Titlows referred to their new summer and week end home as the Stone House. They raised cattle across the road and entertained often. George had an in-ground swimming pool put in the west side yard where many a summer day was spent in the cool clear water.

Stories abound about George Titlow's big personality. His grand niece, Shirley Locke of Uniontown, tells me that when her grandfather died, George kind of took over his grandfatherly duties toward Shirley and her siblings. He visited often and never failed to pass out silver dollars to the children!

Titlow had a huge personality and hung billboards advertising his Titlow Hotel which said, "Eat anywhere you like, but Sleep with Tit!"

One story goes like this: The Titlows threw a big New Years Eve party and at midnight George went out on the front porch and shot off his gun. The next morning he discovered he had killed one of his beef cows. They butchered the poor beast and had another feast.

It is also noted that one of the practical jokes he enjoyed was, when butchering, he would bring a certain long organ to the Titlow Tavern and swing it around, making jokes with his patrons!

Titlow was quite adventurous and was known as the man who brought the first automobile and airplanes to town. He also flew over the Himalayas with Lowell Thomas.

Left to Right: Mrs. George (Anna) Titlow and Edna Craig shade the summer sun as they pose in front of the Stone House.

George Titlow's class reunion was held in the side yard of the Stone House. He is standing to the far left in the back in front of a child who stands on a chair. Circa 1920.

Another shot of the old Stone House. The white gate let visitors into the swimming pool area. About 1915.

Dapper young George Titlow is about 19 years old here.

George Titlow stands in front of the Stone House in the late 1930's.

George Titlow was a generous and compassionate man. In 1903 he bought eighty lots of land on the east side of McClellandtown Road including Thompson, Delaware and Easy Streets. In 1912 he added the Titlow Annex which extended Easy Street eastward to South Mount Vernon Avenue. He later donated most of this property for the building of the Uniontown Hospital and Nurses quarters. Titlow's family home was on McClellandtown Road.

He was also a prosperous, adverturesome, and fun man. Old newspapers mention his name in connection with a variety of events including Old Home Week in 1912, the Summit Mountain Hill Climbs, and the Uniontown Speedway boardtrack.

Titlow was on the Executive Committee and Chairman of the Entertainment Committee for Old Home Week. Meetings were held in the Hotel Titlow for months before the celebration plans for Uniontown's 136th year were complete.

With Titlow in charge of entertainment, it is not surprising that he hired a biplane pilot to fly over Uniontown doing stunts three days in a row. Enormous crowds of residents followed the plane as it dipped, soared and finally landed where the excited folks could walk up and get a good look at the flying machine.

Throughout the week, events like Punch and Judy shows and poetry shows were held in addition to several parades and firemen's contests. The final parade culminated in the crowning of Miss Ina Williams of Collins Street as Queen of Jubilee. This was noted in newspapers as "The most fantastic procession ever witnessed here."

With the streets filled to overflowing, Miss Williams was crowned and granted a diamond ring on the balcony of the McClelland House. She was then escorted by her two attendants to the white Landorf carriage which was adorned with 88 electric lights and purple wisteria. This was pulled by a six horse team contributed by the Pittsburgh Brewing Company, the Uniontown Firemen, and the Hygia Company. Charles Wilkey drove the carriage which led the largest parade in the town's history. Eight firemen trotted alongside the carriage throughout the parade.

3

In 1922 George Titlow, bored with Prohibition, sold his beautiful Hotel Titlow saying, "You can't run a hotel without spirits." He then bought and ran the Hotel George on East Fayette Street and a Dodge dealershop which later became headquarters for the Fayette Chevrolet Company.

George was always known as the man who introduced the automobile to the Uniontown area in 1902. He owned the best horses in the county and proudly served as a volunteer fireman. One of his most prized possessions was a medal he received in 1915 for making a rescue in a downtown fire. He also led the campaign to get J.V. Thompson elected Governer.

In the final five years of his life George lived with his daughter, Mrs. Guy (Orville) Woodward of Washington, Pennsylvania. One day she brought her father into Uniontown to visit his wife's grave at the Oak Grove Cemetery as it was the tenth anniversary of her death. Afterward he made several business calls, one to Attorney Russell Smiley. He then went on to his cousin's office, Judge Henderson. When asked how he'd been Titlow told the Judge he had never felt better. He was in a bit of a hurry as his daughter was waiting for him. "I came by to remind you not to forget the Woodward reunion on June 29," George told him. As the judge turned to mark this date on his calendar, George dropped to the floor. He was buried in the Oak Grove Cemetery in Uniontown at the age of 76.

Deeds show that on February 1, 1912 George sold the Stone House to his wife, Anna for $12,000. 00.This is the price he paid for it before spending thousands on its renovations. We can only speculate here as to why. George is gone. I do know she owned the place until her death in 1930. Daughter MargaretTitlow Robinson sold the Stone House to Reverand James Bouras for $13,000.00 on May 5, 1944. They must have sold parcels before this as Bouras only bought 37.957 acres.

After George's death the restaurant was leased out until they sold it.

Compliments

TITLOW DISTILLING CO.

West Peter Street, rear Titlow Hotel

Distillers of Pure Rye

Leading Brand Uniontown Special

Gallon, $2 to $4

Titlova Palencaren

predava palenko ot

2 do 4 Gallon

George F. Titlow, Jr. - Son of George F. Titlow, Sr., of Uniontown, PA. Born March 29, 1892. Inducted into the military service May 28, 1918. Assigned to Camp Lee, VA. Attached to Infantry Replacements. Commissioned 2nd Lieutenant October 15, 1918, and assigned to the U.S. Cavalry. Honorably discharged February 6, 1919.

Photo and info from "Uniontown's Part in the World War".

The elegant Hotel Titlow lobby was decorated for Old Home Week August 26 - 31, 1912. The uniformed man on the left is the bouncer. who sees that everyone is out of the tavern by 9pm!

The Titlows in Atlantic City, circa 1900

Wife Anna and George load up the pony for a family photo.

George Titlow drives a White Steamer on the Atlantic City, New Jersey beach around 1900. Orville Frey sits beside him. Frey and Titlow both had their names in the cement watering trough on Summit Mountain. Then they called it the Mountain Water Club.

Stone House
1941 - 1946

After their father passed on, the Titlows leased the Stone House to Jack and Ethel Ray. The couple was from Pittsburgh. Jack worked in Uniontown for Rosemary and Hoover,s a truck company. He and his wife lived at the Stone House, ran it as a restaurant, and took in boarders.

Edna Hull Smithberger of Farmington worked for the Rays from 1941 - 1945. The young woman lived in a room off of what is now the Pecan Room. Another waitress from Brownsville, Jane Daniels, occupied a second room next to hers.

The Rays rented out five rooms on the third floor to men who worked drilling gas wells on the Summit Mountain. Edna remembers serving them breakfast every morning, packing their lunches, and then they came back for supper.

Mrs. Ray cooked mainly chicken and steak with the coffee included in the meals. They had one dining room. Today, this smokers dining room is next to the tavern. When you enter the Stone House, the room to the right was used as a living room. The kitchen was in the Pecan room.

There was no tavern at this time. The long front porch wrapped around the sides of the building as Titlow had built it.

During their time here, the Rays adopted a baby daughter named Judy. Mrs Ray was a Hoover, whoose family often visited on holidays. Later, when the Rays moved to Uniontown and Jack passed away, Mrs. Ray took Judy to Pittsburgh to live around her family.

A Mrs. King lived in the white frame house next to the Stone House at this time. The swimming pool was already overgrown.

On November 19,1945 Edna ran off with Kenneth Smithberger to Oakland, Maryland and got married. A man named Denver Pickins officiated the ceremony and the whole thing including license and ring cost $10.00!

On the way back from Oakland, they came to the Stone House and got a room for their honeymoon. Edna continued to work for her room and board, but Kenneth had to pay a whopping $10.00 per week for his.

If you made $10.00 in tips per day, you were very lucky. Sunday was their busiest day, serving homemade noodles and all the trimmings of an old fashioned Sunday dinner. Kenneth was making $45. - $75. per week working six days for Matt McClain and EarlSnyder in Uniontown.

The Smithbergers not only spent their honeymoon here, they dined here recently on their 52nd anniversary. They had chicken and dumplings and a bottle of wine. Think they have a soft spot for the place?

Growing up, Edna and Kenneth were next door neighbors. He lived on the farm that later became Five Pines Campground and she was in the adjacent house. He was a bit shy about asking Edna out. Instead he told his sister if she would go ask Edna to go out with him she could go along! "He would kiss me on the cheek and run," Edna smiles. Edna's brother would follow the couple on their outings. It wasn't long before he got his sister a date so that he could be alone with Edna. After courting for 11 months, they married. She was 24 and he was 21.

Edna kids that he married her days before Thanksgiving so she would cook the Thanksgiving meal for him. "And I been cooking ever since," she laughs. Together they raised five children.

Recently the couple went to see the Titanic, still courting. If they are any indication of the good start the Stone House can give young couples, I would advise others to honeymoon here!

Kenneth remembers he and Jack going to a little store just off Route 40 on Chalk Hill Road every Sunday after dinner for King Edward cigars. Once in a while they went to Braddocks for a couple beers, but not often.

The honeymooners left the Stone House in April of 1946. They moved to Elliotsville and then Farmington and have lived happily ever after. Edna's father, Bill Hull, used to play violin for square dances at the Watering Trough.

Edna Hull, waitress; Ethel Ray, owner; Jane Daniels, waitress, 1941 in the Stone House yard.

Edna says that she and her two brothers and two sisters were picking berries one day on Fayette Springs Road. When they saw buzzards flying around they investigated and ran into a moonshiine still. A bunch of men were sitting around which scared them. The kids ran fast as they could down to the Wharton Furnace. The stil was run by a backwoodser named Harry Anderson. Later, their mother warned them not to go that way and they never did again.

This same Anderson rented a house from Bill Hull. Hull heard rumors that Anderson had a still in the basement. One day he went to collect the rent and said he wanted to see something in the basement. He sent Anderson and his still packing.

Another little story was that Edna had married before Kenneth. She worked at the Stone House then and they honeymooned there, but she says that he was a mama's boy and it didn't last. To this day she never told her Kenneth who it was she had married first! They had only been married a month. Kenneth still tries to get that information from her, but she won't budge.

Mrs. Ray did not want Edna to marry Kenneth. She was a good worker and Ethel did not want to lose her. She followed them around at times and made up stories to tell Kenneth. They had all they could take and found another place to live! Edna never visited her again. Ethel had predicted that the Smithburgers would not last a year!

Edna remembers that Pechin in Dunbar opened up the year they were married.

Kenneth recalls that George Titlow used to light his cigars with 5 dollar bills.

Stone House
Honeymooners

EdnaHull Smithberger and husband Kenneth Smithberger honeymooned at the Stone House in 1945. They recently had their 52nd wedding anniversary dinner at the Stone House. (1998)

Baby Judy Ray is being held by Hoover Grandmother on left.
Jack Ray, Stone House leasee center, Mrs. Jack (Ethel) Ray to
right, Edna Hull looking over Ethel's shoulder.

The Samonas
Years
1944 - 1963

BARON KARL'S STONE HOUSE
on U. S. Route 40   5 Miles East of
Uniontown, Pa.
Dinners A specialty   Nightly Dancing

Stephen Samonas built a tavern by enclosing the left porch. He leased the Stone House to a succession of restaurateurs.

The Rays continued to lease the Stone House for an undisclosed number of years after the Titlows sold it to Reverand James Bouras in May 5, 1944.

On June 13, 1944 the Weirton, West Virginia minister sold the Stone House to Stephen Samonas of Uniontown for $1.00! You can speculate on that if you like. Samonas owned the place until his death when his sister Goldie Samonas Bowles sold it to Fannie Ross in 1963.

Samonas leased the restaurant out to several people through these nineteen years; men named Baron Karl, and Russell Shearer.

Uniontown's General George Marshall in center in black on platform at the 1954 Fort Necessity dedication. He compliments the Stone House chicken & dumplimgs of his youth. "Best I ever tasted," he told his listeners. Fort Necessity is appriximately 1 mile east of the Stone House.

The stories I have gathered concerning the late 1940's and the 1950's show the Stone House tavern as a very busy rowdy place. The Wise boys who lived in the white frame house next door were not allowed to play over here because of all the fights.

They say that one man from Dunbar who leased for two years called the place the "Farmer's Daughter."

As we all know, winters can get very rough on this mountain. We have been lucky recently, but Mother Nature will get us again, no doubt. A story has gone around that the weather was so bad with snow piled high and roads closed; blinding winds and sub zero temperatures, that one leasee burned the tables and chairs from the dining room in the fireplace to keep warm. Business comes to a halt when winter sets in like that!

I have advertised for more information concerning the Stone House restaurateurs from this time frame, but have found out little in the way of fact. Fannie Ross discovered a couple of menus and a wine list, though, and the following lists some of the items and their prices:

Filet Mignon with mushrooms,relish plate, soup, potato, vegetable, salad, dessert, rolls, and coffee...............$3.50!

French Fried Jumbo Shrimp, French Fries & Cole Slaw ...$1.00

Baked Ham Sandwich.................50 cents

From the Bar:
Dry Martini.........................55 cents
Tom Collins........................55 cents
B and B............................75 cents
Calvert Reserve.................40 cents
Old Overholt......................60 cents
Black & White Scotch.........65 cents
Jamaica Rum.....................60 cents
Ales & Beers.....................20 & 25 cents Imported....45
Domestic Wine.................30 cents

Stone House Italian Restaurant 1963 - 1996

Mid 1960's postcard shows they rented rooms. Notice the stone wall that Titlow built to the left of the building is gone.

Biography of Fannie Ross,

W ho never took any crap.

1907 - 2004

On February 20,1964 Fannie Ross and James Cardine bought the Stone House and 37.957 acres from Stephen Samonas' widow, Goldie Samonas Bowles for $20,000.00.

Fannie had attended United Mineworker's Women's Association meetings there in 1932 and 1933. She had come away very impressed with the building and its potential.

Thirty years later, in November 1963, she heard the place was for sale and came to look it over. "She wanted too much money, Honey," Fannie says. "The place needed work. I didn't open up until April. That's how much cleaning it took."

"The mountain people didn't want me up here," she said. "I was an outsider. They did a lot of things trying to get rid of us, but they couldn't."

Who was this little Italian woman from Cardale, Pennsylvania? Why was she impossible to run off?

This is her story:

"I was born in Connellsville in 1907 on the 13th of October. I always say Friday is my good luck day when it comes on the thirteenth. I was born on Friday. My father and mother came from Italy. He was Frances Cassurole and she was Angela Egidi.He was a tailor. I was born by the railroad tracks. There is a song that went:

'It's only a shack by an old railroad track where the roof is so slanted it touches the ground. An old shanty in an old shanty town.'

"My mother and the baby died in childbirth when I was about 3. My brother was about 2. He had infantile paralysis, Joseph did. His son, Carl, works in the courthouse.

"My father got sick and put me and my brother in Saint Paul's Orphan Assylum. It's gone now. I think it burnt. My uncle Chubby was here when my mother died and my father died within six months of her. He wrote to my grandmother in Italy to send one of his sisters over. My mother's sister. Instead Carl decided to take both children back to Italy, but the state wouldn't let him take little Joseph because of his paralysis. So he stayed and the sisters promised they would take care of him. They were curing him by bathing him in water, so Uncle Carl was here about two years when he got permission from the government to take him out. In the meantime his sister Argia had come to this country to help care for mr.He got us a house in Filbert and got her boarders.So, I was 4 or 5 years old when he got permission to take us home to Italy. He got paid every two weeks and he wanted to finish that week off. That morning, his last day in the mines, he had our papers ready and a big trunk packed. My brother still wore stilts.

"He went in the mine that morning and all at once someone came up to the house after me. They called him my father because he adopted us. They said in English that something was wrong with my father. My aunt started to cry and we went down to the mine. My aunt couldn't speak English. While we were with him, he died. It was H.C. Frick's Filbert Mine. They said, 'The fall came in.' It meant the mine collapsed.

"We buried him and we lived with my aunt. She married a Gaily then. Uncle Carl had built us a cellar. It was on a hill. She used to keep all her vegetables in there. He built an outside oven. Neighbors always asked to use her oven, but she didn't allow anyone to use the oven who would put pine in. She baked on Sunday.

"That fall I started to go to school. One of my godfathers took me to school and the teacher asked me my name. I told her in Italian Fenalba Cassurole. She asked how to spell it.

"My aunt told me when someone asks a question you don't know just shrug your shoulders. So I did.Mae Moxley was my first teacher and she had her pencil and tapped it and said, 'Now let's see. We'll call you Fanny. Is that alright?' It was alright with me. I could understand the word alright. I didn't know a lot of English yet. We always spoke Italian.

"That was the Filbert School House. She named me Fannie and I've been Fanny ever since.I went to school there until I was in the 8th grade then I ran away from home. I just didn't like it. She laughs. I went to some Italian friends I knew when Uncle Carl was living. Uncle Chubby came after me and brought me home. I would fight with everybody in school. That was in 1920. I used to get a lot of whippings from Principal Galt.He would put me over the desk and paddle me. I used to play a lot of hookie. I was wild. I should have been a boy. My brother graduated 2nd in his class from German Township High School. My brother had the brains and I had the guts. I wish I would have had both things. Mrs. Maude Peterman was one of my teachers. She used to be a Rankin from the mountains. She always told me I would go far if I had my brother's brains. She knew I was a big tom boy.My aunt and Maude and Mae were good friends.

"When I was a kid I was a paperboy for the Sunday Pittsburgh Dispatch. One day Maude told Uncle Chubby I was real good in arithmetic but rotten in spelling. I would just spell the word how it was pronounced. I left out all silent letters.Uncle Chubby told her that I spell like an Italian-they had no silent letters.

"My brother and I got a pension from H.C. Frick because our Uncle had adopted us and was killed in the mine.So Uncle Chub went to Frick and told him about me. Frick agreed to send me to a good Catholic School. He paid the tuition while my family was to send my clothes. I didn't like girls and I had to go to school with all girls. We were in a dorm. I had never studied religion.

"One day we were taking verbal exams and influenza was all a rage then. A isiter came in with a Catechism this day. She asked everyone questions. I sat there like a dummy because I didn't know anything. Then she asked, 'You, who made you?'

"I said, 'My mother and my father.' Everyone laughed and I got mad. I wanted to know if anyone wanted to dispute that. The sister came to me saying, 'Child, have you ever studied catechism?' I said that I didn't know what that was. So, she said she would tutor me after class. A girl asked if I had ever studied bible history. I said I had history, but not bible history. She told me that I should have answered that God made me. I said that I didn't know he did!

"They asked what I would like to study. I told them cooking and sewing and that kind of stuff. The school was the Monastery of Our Lady of Charity in Pittsburgh.

"Arithmetic was like eating candy for me, you know. It was easy. I did my problems and the sister was surprised. When someone needed to know figures, I helped them out. Then all of a sudden she points her finger at me after writing something on the board and I said that she had her arithmetic mixed up with her alphabet. 'Stay after class', she said, 'I'll tutor you'. 'No!' I got mad and she was being nice. 'Why not child?' I said because I had to get tutored in the other class. She said she would meet me in that class and we worked toward evenings.

"Sisters are rough. They never touched you, but they had other ways of punishing you. Like kneeling on corn. Try that for five minutes. Or try standing with your arms extended for ten minutes. After a while I learned not to get punished. They had bad punishments.

"Then I had to take my First Holy Communion. They had on the board who would be accepted into the convent one day and my name was on the bottom of the list. I was happy I was going home. I was 13 years old. Mother Superior and her helper were listening in on the classes, observing. So, they passed me on the steps and one said to the other, 'What do we do with this child?' 'She's got good brains. We just have to dig into them. She's a challange'. Later I told Mother Superior that I hated her that day. I thought I was going home. She asked me what I would have done? I didn't know. But I had the guts to do almost anything. I was there for six years. I was supposed to go home one month a year, but my family never came after me. They had no car.

"So I stayed at the school. The first year they put me to work rebinding the books and redoing the insides, replacing bad sheets. The second year I thought, good, some one will come after me. Know one was writing to me. My brother was in school and he wasn't writing to me. In fact, I don't even think he knew where I was at. I learned to cook American style. They put me up on a dynamite box to roll the noodles. We cooked with a coal stove. My aunt taught me the Italian cooking. So that second year when no one showed up I wrote to them and got no answer.

"Then when I came home in 1926 I wanted to stay at the school. The sisters said I had to go. I was 17. Uncle Chubby came after me in September. My pension was due to run out when I turned 18 in October. So, I got married to my cousin Decemebr 12, 1926. The marriage was fixed. Joe Ross was much older than me. His mother and my mother's father were brother and sister. They fixed marriages then. When my daughter Tootsie was born my aunt said, 'Oh my, I have a wife for my boy.' I said, 'She can't be your daughter-in-law.'

"I got married in Ralph. That's where my aunt was living when I went home. He got me a house. He bought me what I wanted and we got along real good. But maybe I wanted too much, I don't know. I was spoiled from the convent. The sisters got me my clothes. Uncle Chubby never did. I was used to being taken care of and making money. They taught me to crochet and embroider. Mother Nativity gave me a note. She said to take it down to Murphy's 5 & 10. They sent me to town for things a lot. She said to give the girl at the counter the note. She also gave me 2 dollars. She got me a crochet needle, an embroidery needle, a pair of hoops, thread, and things. I didn't know what I was getting into. But I had enough money to go to a show. It was cheap then. I had ten cents left and bought red lipstick, but Mother Nativity took it off of me. You weren't allowed that stuff. At home she said the things I bought were for me. They taught me then. I did a basket with fruit in it with pretty colors on a table cover, like a long cotton doily. She sold it for me for $5.00 and gave me back $4.00. Each thing I made I gave her a dollar. We sold these things at the 5 & 10.

"Then I went and bought pillow cases and embroidered them all in white. I got $10.00 for them and thought I was rich! I never saw the money Frick sent for my tuition. They gave me 50 cents a month and later a dollar a month, but this! It took me two weeks to do all the work while still doing my studies. I made a beautiful 2 inch wide crochet pattern on them. By the time I came home from the convent I had $200.00. Uncle Chubby wanted to know where I got that money. I said that I worked for it. When we got married we moved from Ralph to Filbert. My uncle had a pool room . He was bootlegging from there. He made wine and beer. My aunt used to make wine and beer and men would come into the kitchen table and drink during prohibition. They came on Saturday nights and played cards. She sold a lot of rum.

"When I got married I saw that my husband wasn't bringing me in any money. He was a gambler, too. Most times he didn't win. He worked at Filbert Mine. We bought our furniture at Cohen's and every two weeks they would come and collect. My husband would leave me the money for the payments and food. One week he didn't leave me any and the collector came. I said my husband forgot to leave me the money. The next two weeks, same thing. I didn't have any money. The third time I went upstairs and hid. My aunt came up after he left and said, "Why didn't you open the door?' I said Joe wasn't leaving the money. She said she would give me all three payments and I was to go the next day and pay the bills. She said not to tell Joe, she would take care of it. She met him when he was at the pay station next to the company store. She told him to help her with her packages. He did. When they got to her house she said he owed her $20.00 for those payments. They were cousins, too. She got the money off of him and said that he would lose Fannie if he didn't straighten up. Fannie left him, but they got back together. He promised to be different, but he wasn't. I decided we were getting along allright at home. The depression came and the men were only getting $5.00 a day in the mine.

"I went to a friend of mine and told him what the trouble was. First thing you know I got a letter to meet someone in Uniontown. The next two days I had 5 gallon of moonshine and the bottles. I

"I bartered for a lot of the stuff. The single men were getting sacks of food. The govenment was giving them beans, and ham hocks, and butter. I would give them half a pint of moonshine to get their beans. Or a pint for 25 pounds of flour. I was penny pinching. The moonshine and bottles were given to me in the beginning to get me started. Twice they gave it to me. They brought it in from Philadelphia. The third time I paid $5.00 for 5 gallons and sold it for 50 cents a pint. I made money on it and moved from one house to another. I was bootlegging real good. In the new house there used to be a post office, so I put a little confectionary store in. I was selling candy, and beer, and moonshine, and I was hording the money. I'd buy the malt in the company store. Now this is what gets me. They sold the malt to you, but if you sold it you'd get caught. But I never got caught bootlegging. I got caught gambling. This was on Main Street in Cardale. I paid $2,000.00 for the 8 room house. Then I bought the house next to it for $2,500.00. It had been a bowling alley, but they tore it down and made it into a house. It had a cellar and garage downstairs and I made a wine cellar. There was a shower and bathroom downstairs and a kitchen. We made a place to gamble right on Main Street. I liked it because it was in between an alley. Cars could park in the back. I rented the one house and lived upstairs in the other and ran my business downstairs. That's where I got raided for gambling. I served 6 months in the work house and cooked for the warden. They gave me a gift when I left the place. Once a week auditors came in and I was making spaghetti. The auditors requested I make it every Thursday when they came! I had taken $100.00 when I went in, but never spent it. This was Blawnox in Allegheny County, 1939. I got home January 1940.They took my husband, too. He had been dealing. Uncle Chubby watched my two children and they went to Filbert School until I got out. When young Carl went to Filbert School that first day the teacher asked if that was Fannie's boy. Uncle Chubby said he was. The teacher replied that she hoped she didn't have the trouble with him she had with his mother! I guess I was hard, Fannie laughs.The warden gave Fannie gifts of money for her fine cooking when she left. She went straight to the liqour store!

About two months later a friend got sent there and Fannie went to see him. The warden asked Fannie what she did with the $300.00 she left there with. Fannie told him he didn't want to know. "I had stopped at my Uncle's and ordered beer and went to the liquor store and purchased all whiskey. There were 3 or 4 guards with him and they laughed. "You'll never learn," the warden said. "I don't want to," she told him.

"I sold shots for 10 cents and bottles of beer for 10 cents. I had miners from Allison who came every Sunday. They came in two car loads and pulled around back so no one could see them. They never left until each one bought a round. There were ten of them!

In the 1940's Fannie opened the Coffee Pot on Route 40 in Brier Hill.

She moved to Cleveland, Ohio in 1950 after her husband died of black lung. Her daughter lived there. Fannie bought a big house. Many men from Cardale who frequented her Speak Easy were out there working. She boarded them. One worked at the Plain Dealer newspaper. She had a restaurant away from her house called Nights in Paris. Then her friend Gene Cardine came out to stay at Fannie's. They ran two restaurants and the boarding house, bootlegging all the while. On week ends they played cards and drank in the basement.

In 1962 Fannie heard the Stone House was for sale. She called a Real Estate man in Herbert. He showed her a place in Brownsville that was for sale, but she and Gene didn't like it. The next week they looked at the Stone House. It was called the Farmer's Daughter and run by Russ Spearer. Wise's lived in the frame house next door.

"Samonas had sold the parquet floors to the Titlow girls. With the money he made out of that, he enclosed the porch and made a tavern. There was someone from Dunbar, someone from Cleveland, Ohio, then Russ Shearer who rented from Samonas.

"I needed good insurance for the place, so I had to move the kitchen. In 1975 I put the new kitchen in." In 1974 Gene (James) Cardine, Fannie's long time friend and partner died of a massive heart attack and her son Carl camehome to help her run things.

Gene Cardine was a man with a sense of humor. He and Fannie ran the Stone House together for 10 years until his death. He left to pick up supplies one day andonly got to Chalk Hill when he pulled off the road into a ditch. His dog Fang was in the car, but would not let anyone near them. Fannie came up and coaxed the dog out of the automobile, but Gene was gone. "Take me, not my man," Fannie cried.

Left to right: Waitress Millie Pascanik and Gene Cardine pose for a promotional picture for Kesslar's liquor in the early 1970's.

Fannie's Italian Stone House fed more travelers than anyone can count. Her homemade lasagne, spaghetti sauce, bread, and gnocchi's were a hit. Here, Fannie's son Carl and she work bread dough. Carl's son Carl is in the background working alongside them in the early 1980's.

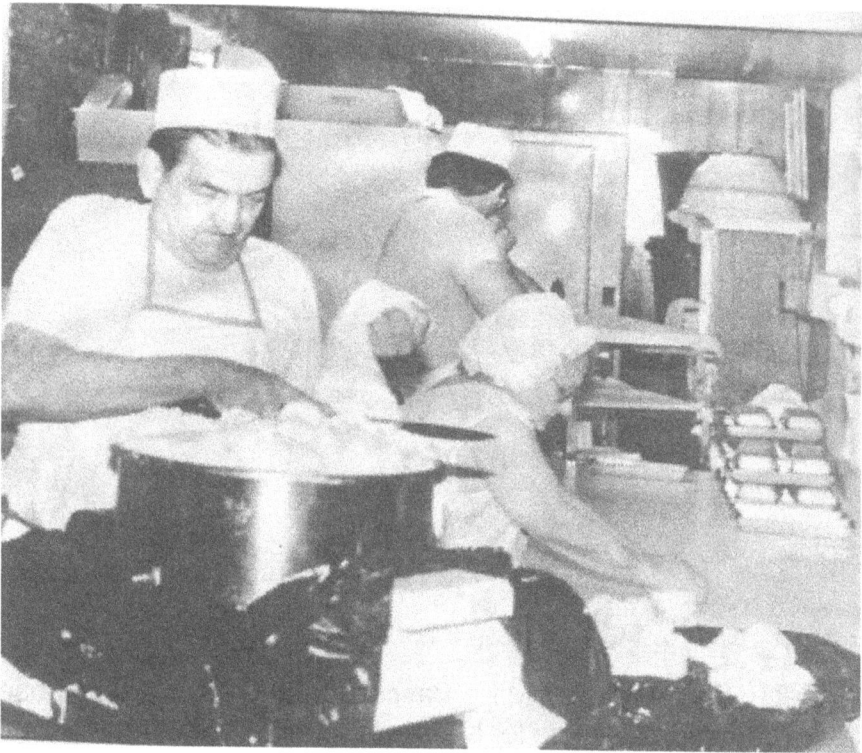

Carl Ross wrote the following on a placemat that they used on tables for years:

History of the Stone House

The Stone House has been here since shortly after the National Road opened for traffic between Baltimore and Wheeling in 1811. It was constructed by the same stone masons who constructed the bridges along the highway. For over fifty years the National Road was practically the Main Street of America inviting the east to the vast territories west of the Allegheny Mountains.

George Washington first advocated the building of the National Road. In 1806 Congress passed a bill "to build a road from the navigable waters of the Atlantic to the river Ohio." This bill was signed by Thomas Jefferson, March 29th, 1806. Army engineers surveyed the road, constructed bridges, many of which are still standing, and superintended the building of the highway. For many years it was a tollroad with an almost constant stream of traffic in both directions.

Statesmen, soldiers, politicians, merchants, tradesmen, immigrants, horses, cattle-all used the road. There were brightly painted stage coaches, Conestoga wagons loaded with goods for the west and produce for the east; there were sulkies, chaises, phaetons, carts; indeed every known kind of wheeled vehicle rolled over this highway. Associated with its story are linked the names of George Washington, Benjamin Franklin, Thomas Jefferson, General Braddock, Alexander Hamilton, General Light-Horse Harry Lee, General LaFayette, James Monroe, John Quincy Adams, Andrew Jackson, General Sam Houston, William Henry Harrison, Zachary Taylor, James C. Fremont, Abraham Lincoln, Robert E. Lee, Davy Crocket, Santa Anna, Chief Blackhawk, Stonewall Jackson, George Gordon Meade, Jeb Stuart, P.T. Barnum, Jenny Lind, and a host of others, many of whom stayed overnight at the Stone House.

As a guest of this old inn you are close to three great historical sights. A few miles to the northwest is Jumonville Glen where George Washington-on May 28th, 1754- received his baptism of fire. There he killed or captured a French force of thirty seven under Captain LaForce. A mile to the east is the grave of General Edward Braddock, and a mile farther on is Fort Necessity, a National Battlefield site where Lt. Colonel George Washington on July 3rd, 1754 fought his first battle against a large force of French and Indians. This battle marked the beginning of the French and Indian War in America and the Seven Years War in Europe. We hope you have enjoyed your visit and look forward to your stopping in again.

Carlo Ross.

Fannie's Stone House's Main Dining Room. Notice the whiskey decanters along upper wall ledges.

For thirty one years, Fannie got up and began cooking by 6 am. Her secret spaghetti sauce was stirred gently through the wee hours while prying eyes were sleeping.

She and Gene moved into the building January 1, 1964. They cleaned their new home and business from top to bottom before opening in April of 1964. Fannie made homemade ravioli, spaghtti, and gnocchis. The ravilois were so impossible to keep up with, she began making lasagne instead.

"They were more intersted in my spaghetti, lasagne, and gnocchi. Those are my big sellers. And my roguefort dressing. In 1973 Gene wanted to sell. 'It's too much work', he said. I said, 'I don't care.' He died that year of a cerebral hemorage.

"I had a lot of friends and they came to see me. It was tough at first. I was blamed for things I didn't do. They questioned me when the Ohiopyle Hotel burnt and the Chalk Hill House. The manager from the Chalk Hill House was here eating when it happened. I sold spaghetti all you could eat for $2.00 in the beginning. They didn't know about having an Italian place up here. Once they ate here, though, they came back. People told each other about it.

Her menu remained pretty constant throughout her rein. You could order your steak whatever thickness you liked. Carl cut them to order. Sundays you could count on homemade chicken noodle soup and prime rib. If you were lucky, she'd sell you a loaf of her wonderful Italian bread. Fannie worked hard and she was good to her help. She built work ethic in those who understood her rough ways and rewarded them with friendship and supper.

On Sundays Fannie sat at her cash register in the front lobby. She greeted everyone with a 'How are you, honey.' and proceeded to yell out orders to her bus help and waitreses as to where to seat the nice folks. She'd ask about the family and really cared. I still expect her to be sitting there when I walk in.

When Gene passed on in 1973 Fannie's son and his family moved home to help keep the business going. Carl and Fannie became a team and ran a welcoming clean place. In 1995 both their healths became so strained that they closed the restaurant, running only the tavern.

"First they took my tit and then my legs wouldn't work, and now I choke all the time." Fannie left the Stone House under protest. She wanted to live out her life there, but her body wouldn't co operate any longer. It makes her frustrated and angry, but she is happy with the choice she made in new proprieters.

Several buyers had come along during the last few years of her running the restaurant, but she wanted someone who would care about the place like she did, to own it. The Stone House was built by an amazing man. George Titlow was a strong character, and she herself had strength enough for ten men in that short wide body. She had no intentions of selling to the first or highest bidder just to unload it. This was her home.

When local entreprenuer Fred Zeigler began speaking with her about acquiring the Stone House, she knew she had her man. "That Fred, I like him. He has guts. If I was thirty, there wouldn't be anyone who could get him away from me." She liked Fred's energy and trusted he would do right by the Stone House, where she left her heart.

It took Carl and Fannie well over a year to clean out their four floors of room after room. Fannie was from the old school. She saved things. They came in handy. But moving when you are a saver, is an enormous job. Several times, Carl called me and said, 'Mom wants you to stop in. She found something for you.' Fannie donated the following items to my Yesteryear Museum from the things she found during the move: a charcoal portrait of George Titlow, a large photograph of over 100 soldiers from the Spanish American War taken in 1899, over four hundred rare books she had read, a large book shelf for the books, photographs of the Sone House, a huge meat scale used by the Titlows when they raised beef, and more.

Fannie is 90 years old and lives in Hopwood with her son, Carl. She is thrilled that Fred Zeigler has invested in the renovation of her precious Stone House. A fine example of the kind of loyalty Fannie possesses is this: When Fannie was in the lawyer's office signing the deed over to Fred and Rhonda Zeigler, another buyer offered her $25,000.00 over Zeigler's price. She passed.

Fannie, Get Your Gun

I met Fannie in 1978 when I came to work for her for the summer. "I liked you right away," she tells me. "Ever since that first day when those guys were hassling you and you told them to go --- themselves." We laughed over that. Most employers would fire a person for that. Not Fannie. She believed in standing your ground and respected those who did. Being a small woman (wearing a size 4 shoe) in a rough business all her life, she had to defend herself more than once.The miners got out of hand in her Cardale Speak Easy one time and Fannie told them to keep it down. Her husband was ill and trying to sleep. One of the men hit Fannie and they got into it. He knocked her down in back of a booth and she found a bottle and broke it. She went after him and they fought more. Then he kicked her dog. "He kicked my dog who was trying to help me. That made me mad. I went behind the bar and got the gun and shot him in the pelvis. "Another time I had a little place called the Coffee Pot on Route 40 and this manwouldn't pay his bill, so I shot him. I was good friends with the state police. There was about six of them from Keister. They were drunk and I had two of my friends sitting at a table. They had burgers and didn't wanna pay the bill. I told them, 'You pay the bill or else.' 'Or else what?' one of the asked.' I didn't even take the gun out of my pocket. I just shot him.' She hit him pretty close to the groin area. Then she called the police and that night around 2am they stopped at the door. They said it wasn't reported at the hospital and they went away. The next morning Officer Steinmeyer came in when I was punching bread and a man came in who wanted to see the boss. Steinmeyer opened the refrigerator and got a piece of pie and put it on the counter. He asked the man what he wanted-Fannie is busy kneading her dough. He said he wanted to know who shot his boy the last night. The cop asked him who was going to clean up the damage as the men had turned over a table. The cop said he tried to rob this woman, didn't want to pay.

"It turned out that the boy who got shot told the doctor that he was walking down the road and someone shot him from a car.

One time a car load of young men stopped late at night at the Stone House. They wanted to use the phone, but Fannie wouldn't let them in. She called her son who lived a few miles down the road in Farmington. Carl came and gave one of the guys a ride to Hopwood to get some gas. Fannie told the rest of them to stay in their car while Carl did them the favor. One of the men challanged her and came toward her in an unfriendly manner. She shot him in the foot.

The Stone House Tavern was never a rough place when Fannie owned it. If someone got out of hand, Fannie would get the gun out and tell them not to come back. This got around and after a while, she didn't have to get the gun out anymore.

"I was having fun. I love a good fight, but not in my Stone House."

Fannie says that Gene asked her when they were opening the place what she wanted to call it. "What it is, the Stone House," she told him.

And the Stone House it is.

Millie Pascanik, Waitress Extraordinaire

Millie Pascinik began working for Fannie in 1966. After thirty two years, Millie still fills the Stone House with laughter.

"I met Fannie down at the Hopwood laundromat one day. She couldn't get over how much clothes I had with the eight kids. I would have bushels and bushels. She was so happy to meet me because I was Italian. She was happy there was another Italian family in the mountains. So, she asked me to come to work for her. I said, 'What do I do? I don't know how. I never worked for anybody before.' She said to just come. So I started out as a dishwasher then I went to making salads. I used to put out the prettiest antipastas. Then from there, Gene said to help him at the steam table. Then she put me out in the dining room and would never let me back in the kitchen again."

That was a good move on Fannie's part. Millie is a natural on the floor. Her sense of humor and warmth has welcomed thousands of diners and keeps them coming back.

"It's nice to make peolpe laugh, but if it wasn't for her good food... Gene was the most kind man you ever wanted to meet and Fannie was so stern for the longest time. She used to rule that Stone House with an iron fist. You had to keep it clean. She used to go around with a white glove to see if we dusted. But Gene was the man. She made her homemade gnocchi and ravioli's everyday. She couldn't keep up with the ravioli because they were so good. I suggested to her to make lasagne instead, so she did. Between the lasagne, gnocchis, and homemade fettucini...She made the best.

"Some nights when I didn't have a babysitter I would take my kids with me. Susie, Jeanie, and Peter came with me. She started Susie cleaning dishes in the kitchen. Fannie would put a few dollars away for her. My girls used to call Gene 'Daddy Gene'. They just loved him. "Fannie would never get her picture taken, so I always had to take pictures with Gene. During the day he did the shopping and she got everything ready. Then he went in the kitchen and she took care of the bar starting supper hours. When she got an order for a whiskey sour she would make a little extra and save me a shot of it. When I started slurring my words in the dining room I told her she better cut irt out. "It's been quite an experience. It's been my home away from home for the last thirty years.

And my children's home. I quit one time for six months to help my husband paint, but I came back. My most memorable year was when they made a movie in the mountains about George Washington. Stars came in from Hollywood. It was the year Joan Baez' song was so popular, 'The Night they Drove Old Dixie Down.'

"We waited on movie stars, all the extras. George Montgomery, one of the men who always played the District Attorney on Perry Mason, Tagart I think. And one of the men from Benson, the tall secretary. I waited on a lot of television personalities and judges, lawyers from Uniontown. They were here all summer. Very good time and good tips.

"The extras used to come to the bar at night and when that Joan Baez song came on they would all sway back and forth at the bar and sing.

Dan and Millie Pascanik relax at the Stone House Tavern, 1974.

"But the general public are the stars to me. They've kind of become good friends with me. We kind of adopted each other. They keep coming back year after year. I've seen a lot of their little children grow up and they still come back. I've made a lot of friends. We have regulars that come in from all over-Pittsburgh, Maryland, they just keep coming back.

"Fannie and I got along right away because we were both from the same Italian heritage." When Zeigler bought the place in 1996 Millie stayed on, but had a hard time mastering the computer system. "It was a big change. I took two days of it and I quit. I couldn't handle the computers.

"One day my family and I were up for dinner and Fred talked me into coming back. He said he'd put me on days when it would be slower and they would work with me. I said, 'OK, I'll try it.' I did come back and learned day by day. Everday you learn something on those computers, you know. I was not used to them. I worked without computers for the last 28 years and then these computers show up, but, Oh, my God, they're so easy. They do everything for you whereas we used to have to add all our bills before.

"I was there for about a month when I fell in the kitchen. A waitress spilled soup and I slid right through it and tore a hamstring and I was out for about six weeks. That was painful. After I healed and got better I came back and here I am today!

"Fannie had never even taken charge cards until the last year or so. Her granddaughter, Angie got her to because so many people asked. "Fannie took personal checks and cash. She was a cash oriented person.

"Her and I, we kinda had a routine. After a while I kind of mellowed her out. There wasn't a day when you didn't laugh in that building. Her and I used to have fun. She had an operation on one of her breasts. And she would take off her fake one and not remember where she put it. So, when we had a dining room full of people she would yell, 'Hey, Millie, have you seen my tit laying around?' I'd say, 'I think it's right there Fanny and this guy has gravy all over it!'

"We used to laugh all day long there. Gene had a great sense of humor. We would play 'Name that Tune' when that show was popular. But once in a while he would make up a song and trick us.

"He was going into town one day to get onions and pulled on the side of the road up on by Chalk Hill Lodge. No one could get near the car because his dog, Fang, was with him. Those two were inseperable. Every place he went the dog went. Finally me and Fanny went up. She coaxed the dog out of the car. She cried, 'Not my man. Take me. Don't take my man.'

"After that, her son Carl brought his wife and children here from Ohio to help his mother run the place.

"My daughter, Diane, lived there for a while. She used to help out every week end and on Mother's Day. A couple of my children worked with me there. After I started waiting tables in the dining rooms Susie did salads and Jeanie did desserts. Diane would work with me in the dining room. Danny was the bus boy. Michael used to clean the bar.

"And waitresses used to come and go. They'd come in and the next day they'd be gone. Couldn't handle Fannie's sternness. I broke you in. I broke a lot of waitresses in. I used to have to break in the cooks, too, since I had worked in all the sections.

"Madeline started one Mother's Day and then started to cook. She was there a long time. My friend Betty Galloway worked with me. We got to be family. After a while we got to be close people with each other and there wasn't anything we wouldn't do for each other. We looked after each other.

"Fannie and Gene tended bar, but on the week end she would have her cousin come up. Then as time went, on she hired women bartenders.

"She ran the place with an iron fist and everything had to be perfect. She used to holler and bang that bell and bang it on the desk yelling, 'Get your----up here.' Dear.

"When I first started there I made $6.00 a day for an 8 hour shift. That was for dishwasher. And as salad girl I got $6.00. Then as time went on things got a little different with minimum wage. We got a litttle more money. It was tough in the beginning .

Millie enjoys her work and entertains customers with jokes, some her own. Fannie says Millie missed her calling. She should have had an agent to manage her comedy career, but Millie feels blessed. She married the man she loved. She has 8 children to love, and she has the Stone House as her stage. Those who have the pleasure of her service are blessed.

Fannie Ross, Easter Sunday, April 12, 1998. Fannie laughs as she talks about Millie's comedic talent. "She missed her calling, honey."

"This year they named a dinner after me. Chicken Amelia. It's been going pretty good. It's stuffed chicken with rice. I tell Carl, 'When I serve Chicken Amelia and they take the first bite my body starts moving and moving and moving and then when they get to the bone I go, *Ahh!*' Yea, I was there so many years, I'm honored.

"Lot of memories there. Fannie ever tell you there are ghosts upstairs? She used to tell me there are ghosts upstairs. Somebody was killed upstairs in one of the bedrooms. Go up the stairs. The left room. It's a nice big room. Years and years ago. Shot. They claimed the blood stain is there under the rug. Fannie used to tell me she would hear ghosts walking around and she would tell them, 'Hey, if you can't get a dust rag and clean while I'm sleeping, get the hell out!' And they all left. She was good at everything!

"She made a go of it. One week end Gene hired two men to cook. They were Mario and Juan. They came to work Friday night. I had to show them around the kitchen and so forth. They had a slang, hollering out orders-like-'ok, we got spaghetti in the well'. I would yell back, 'If Fannie hears you got spaghetti in her well, you're gona get it. You're gona clog up all the water pipes.' They would toss steaks to each other. And they were putting garlic sauce on everything that came out of that kitchen. I told him Fannie was going to get mad, so Sunday night came around. That was pay day. Gene paid them and told them they wouldn't be needing them anymore. They drove me nuts. They made a buttery garlic sauce and put it on everything. She took a shit fit. They lasted 3 days. I had to watch everybody.

"One night we were really very busy in the dining room and I had a table of gentlemen. They ordered their dinner and I brought their salads out, and their drinks. This one gentleman says to me, 'Millie, my milk is sour. I got him another glass and brought it back. Then When I brought their dinners out he said he didn't want it. Fannie saw me bringing his plate back in the kitchen and asked what was wrong with that spaghetti. I told her about the milk and now the spaghetti. You have to picture this. The dining room is full of people. Everybody's fork is up and their eating. She stands in that doorway going into the oak room with a meat cleaver in her hand at her side and says real loud, "Which table was it, Millie?' I said, 'Right over there, Fannie.' Everything got quiet and theyre all looking at Fannie. Boom. Boom. Boom. She walks to the table and he is watching her now. You have to picture this with everyone holding their forks in mid air. She goes, 'What's the big idea giving my head waitress a hard time? Just because you didn't get laid last night doesn't mean you can take it out on her. Millie, add up what he ate and give him the bill. She turned to him and said, 'And you get the f--- out.' She turns around and says to the dining room, 'And everybody better eat their dinner'. Their forks were busy going up and down then! This guy sitting with him told him he had finally met his match. He must of been a person who was hard to get along with on a regular basis.

"She stuck up for us and taught us that the customer is not always right.

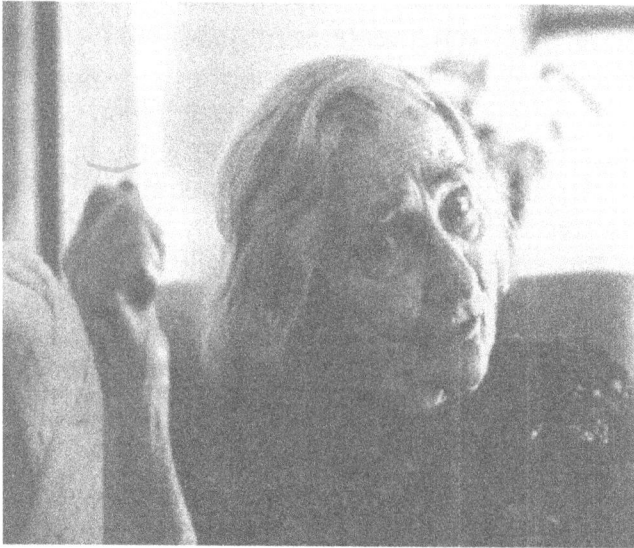

Fannie Ross tells of one day taking a very long rolling pin after a teacher when her daughter, Tootsie, came home with her knuckles broke open from the teacher's pointer. The teacher is not always right, either.

"You have to keep the customers happy. They pay their bill gladly.

"A lot of the girls I trained still come to see me. They're like family to me. I am 70 years old and I love it. I don't know what I would do with myself if I didn't work at the Stone House. I love the public. I love people. I like to make them laugh and glad they're healthy. I'm having a good time. The time of my life.

"I like having men and women servers. I keep them straight. I get them. Make them blush. You really don't mind working hard when you are having a good time."

Fannie Ross gives advice. "Don't get stuck with the first man you love. Date them all so you see what"s what."

Stone House Experience - 1968

"I was 18 and graduated from high school. I got a job at a shirt factory downtown and had worked at the Stone House since I was 14 off and on. When Fannie found out how many kids Mom had, we started working there. We needed the money. We were making salads and things in the kitchen. I was living in town, but wanted to move.

"I was a little intimidated by Fannie. One day Mom (Millie) told me that she mentioned to Fannie that I was looking for a place to live. Fannie said I could live there. I had to help out and she charged me no rent. So I went up. I had my own car. We decided I would work my keep. You never went hungry living there. I worked my job down town and cleaned Fannie's bar and restrooms and the floor I lived on. I lived on the second floor. I got up 5 o'clock in the morning and it worked out well. I did that for a year. Sunday nights I would go out. We closed at 8 o'clock and we'd go to West Virginia. We'd stop at the hot spots. It was a time when we protested the Vietnam War. You didn't know how to take people. You'd get into discussions about the war. One Sunday night I met my husband at the White House in Smithfield. He had just got back from a tour in Viet Nam. I told Fannie about him and showed her a picture and told her he was Italian. Fannie made a rule. He had to come there to pick me up. She got on the phone with him one day and gave him a good talking to. He wanted to know who the hell that was! She is from the old world and treated me like a daughter.

"Gene told me war stories and was impressed that Mike was in the war. Then they found out they knew his relatives and everything was good.

"Fannie wanted to know how often he was coming home because I had responsibilities- with two jobs. They kept me busy I was getting only 5 hours sleep. I said he didn't get leave very often and she said , 'Good, then you won't get pregnant.'

"Her and I had really deep discussions about sex. Her and Gene treated me like their kid. It was a really good family.

"I have to say that she taught me how to handle people. And how to create a good work ethic for my life. It has stuck with me.

"I was 13 when we moved from Pittsburgh to the mountains. I watched my parents go from wealth to poverty in 5 years time. And it was hard because we were Catholic. The bigotry and hatred was a problem. We were outcasts. We had a tough time up there, but she took us in and knew everybody.

"She and Gene had a very strong work ethic. They would always tell us, "You're not getting anywhere sitting on your ----.'

"She would scream and yell. When we first started working down there my father didn't like that. He said it was no way to treat employees. Mom would tell him to chill out. She was nice to us. It bothered him that she was so hardcore. He said she should be in the Army. Fannie didn't take any crap off of anyone. And you do it her way or no way. Once you got past that-because she'd be screaming at you and calling you every filthy name in the book on one hand-and then she'd hand you spaghetti and tell you to eat, but just do it my way.

"We were never allowed to touch the bread or make any specialties. My husband is a plumber and she would call him to come up and do work for her. He said that she had the cleanest kitchen he had ever been in. She is meticulous.

"If she would see dirt around the leg of the stove she would flip out. She was close to the ground, too. She could see it. She didn't want any dirt around her food. You wore a hairnet when you worked. You washed your hands. Once you knew this you would train the people that came in. She said the worst thing you could see was hair in your food."

"She instilled in many of her workers a strong work ethic. She said if you are going to succeed in life, you better live by a set of rules. If you go either way on those rules you're not going to get where you want to go. She taught me not to take crap off of any- body. She would say to stand your ground and if anybody gets in your way, just shoot them! (Diane hasn't gone that far.)

"The nuns that raised her came up to see her a lot. They taught her to be a diciplinarian. Fannie wondered why they came to see her-she had been so much trouble.

"When Gene and Fannie came to your home they never came without food. They were more at ease away from the restaurant, too. Less stress. Gene said Fannie's roughness was what attracted him to her. He was gentle.

"When Mike and I decided to get married Fannie offered to have the reception at the Stone House. She and Mom made all these Italian cookies. Fannie decorated the whole first floor. It was beau- tiful. They did some awful nice things for us. Gene helped us get our first house.

"Off and on I continued to work for her until she closed. The wait staff up there was fabulous. She always hired friends. They all busted their---. And you cleaned up when you were done.Every person cleaned every night. You scrubbed those pots and pans until they shined. And sometimes they were soooo dirty.

"They kept leaving the big pots for me. When I would get home from that 110 degree hot box I had to scrub these huge pots. One day I asked fannie why they left them for me. She hadn't paid at- tention, but yelled, 'Terry!' It was Terry Wise.He was the dish- washer then. Terry grew up there. One night he was about ten or eleven and he was the gopher. He was the only one brave enough to go in the basement because there were snakes down there.. One day he came up with some cans of tomato puree and he hit the sugar bag. He dumped the whole bag. I thought it was World War III. She came back in that kitchen and saw that sugar on the floor. It was 25 lb. of sugar. She was screaming at him calling him every name in the book. She made him pick up that sugar with a beer cap and put it back in that bag to throw it away-not sweep it with a broom. She said that if he can't be careful he'll have to learn how to be careful. He has to learn. It took him a good 2 1/2 hours to do it. He got out of work for a while. Then she said, 'Honey, sit down. You did a good job, now sit down and eat your dinner.' He ate and went home. He didn't think anything of it. The wait staff was shocked.

"Gene just said, 'Oh, boy, look what you did. He would come in and say, 'Give me some sugar for my coffee.'

"People were scared to death around his dog, Fang, but Fannie would tell them he wouldn't hurt them. I worked with my mother a lot on the floor. Fannie worked the bar and it was all open. They had Italian beads hanging down and Fannie listened to everything. On occassions when customers would give us a hassle she always told us not to argue with the customers. We were to just go get her if she wasn't already there. They would ask to see the manager and she would be standing behind you. They wouldn't realize she was the manager. She would be walking through in her apron. She would physically throw people out and tell them to never come back if they would eat their dinner and then complain about it. She would say, 'Sure you son of a -----. You eat the food and then complain about it' while she was throwing them out. Then she's tell me that that's the way to handle them. And people in the restaurant would just look at her and keep eating. But Fannie was nice to the nice people. Up to the day they shut down, it was a fun experience.

"Gene always said when they first bought the restaurant they had bands and dancing and all-you-can-eat spaghetti for a buck 98. It got them off the ground. There weren't too many Italians up here then. They thought if you were Italian you were in the mob. She drew them in slowly. All of a sudden word got out about her food.

And the rafting business was getting off the ground in a big way, then. That helped a lot.

"I never saw a woman who had as much energy as she did. She would work you under the table. The day Gene died was a horrible tragedy. It was like losing your right arm, but she carried on that business. Then she got breast cancer and got that fake tit. She hated that thing.

"They got it all and gave her a clean bill of health. After she got her strength back she sat at the cash register on Sundays.

"Once in a while someone would leave without paying and the waitress would have to pay for that meal. Heaven forbid if they should come in again. One day that happened and I pointed them out to Fannie. She whipped out that gun and put it to this man's head and said, 'Get the f--- out and don't you ever walk in this restaurant again. Never.' You didn't walk out on her.

"When she got her health back she got all prettied up and came out that Sunday and I told her how nice she looked, I fixed her tit. It was crooked. She said real loud, 'Get your hand off my fake tit. You know I don't like this. It looks phoney. One's perky and one's sagging.' People were coming in and she keeps b------ing about it. All of a sudden she reached up her sleeve and was messing around in there. The place was packed and she pulled that titty off, stuffed it in a drawer, and said she wouldn't wear it anymore. If people didn't like a one-titted broad, too bad. The whole place cracked up

"She is a character. Her and Gene were always joking. He would kid her a lot. They were caring people. She has a very good heart. That's what I most ly think of about Fannie- and energy, and determination. Some people might not think that, but I know different. You have to know the person behind that roughness. She was a single woman and that was her business. She protected it.

"And I've never seen a woman with such a positive attitude as my mother. Her and Fannie were a pair. They had great fun.

"Fannie wanted women to stand up for their rights. That impressed me about her being from that generation. A lot of women hated her, but she earned her respect and taught us, also. I didn't understand the lesson she was teaching me until later. I knew if I could work for her, I could work for anybody.

"She told me that the only person you can trust is youself, because you know what you want and where you want to go.

Terry Wise -

Growing up at the Stone House

Terry Wise moved into the frame house next to the Stone House with his family when he was 3 months old. That was 1958. He started working for Fannie when he was a small boy. Around 6 or 7 years old. He got a quarter a day for cleaning and sweeping the porch and cleaning up out front. " My next job was cleaning the bar and kitchen and scrubbing floors. I got in trouble one time for not cleaning under the stove. She made me lay down and stood on my back while I did it right. I was about 12 or 13. I bussed tables until I was 18.

"Gene got me out of a lot of trouble with Fannie. I did everything. I only saw him mad one time at some drunk in here. He'd do anything for you. He was like a kid. They both ran the bar. Fannie had a stool over in the corner by the wall.

"I've never seen any ghosts here. I heard stories, but I can't say if they're true or not.

"One time I was sitting there and she went to the rest room. She came back out and wanted to know what I was doing sitting there. I said I was watching TV. She had 2 silver dollars in her apron and she hit me on top of the head with them.

Terry remembers that before Fannie bought the place there were alot of fights. He wasn't allowed to play out front. Throughout his life he helped Fannie daily. When she couldn't find him she would yell out the back door, 'Terry, boy. Where's my Terry boy?'

"I used to sleep a lot here. I used to sneak off and sleep any place I could. I slept under the beds and the tables. Fannie has a picture of me sleeping on the floor with two dogs. I'm in between them.

Terry moved at least a hundred truck loads out of the Stone House when Fannie moved. He still helps her with chores on Sundays at her house in Hopwood.

The photograph below shows the Stone House in 1996 just before the Rosses sold to the Zeiglers. Fannie had closed the restaurant the last year she lived there, but Carl still ran the tavern. Carl's Cadillac sits out front. The sign tells a sad tale. "Restaurant Closed."

Carl Ross - 1996

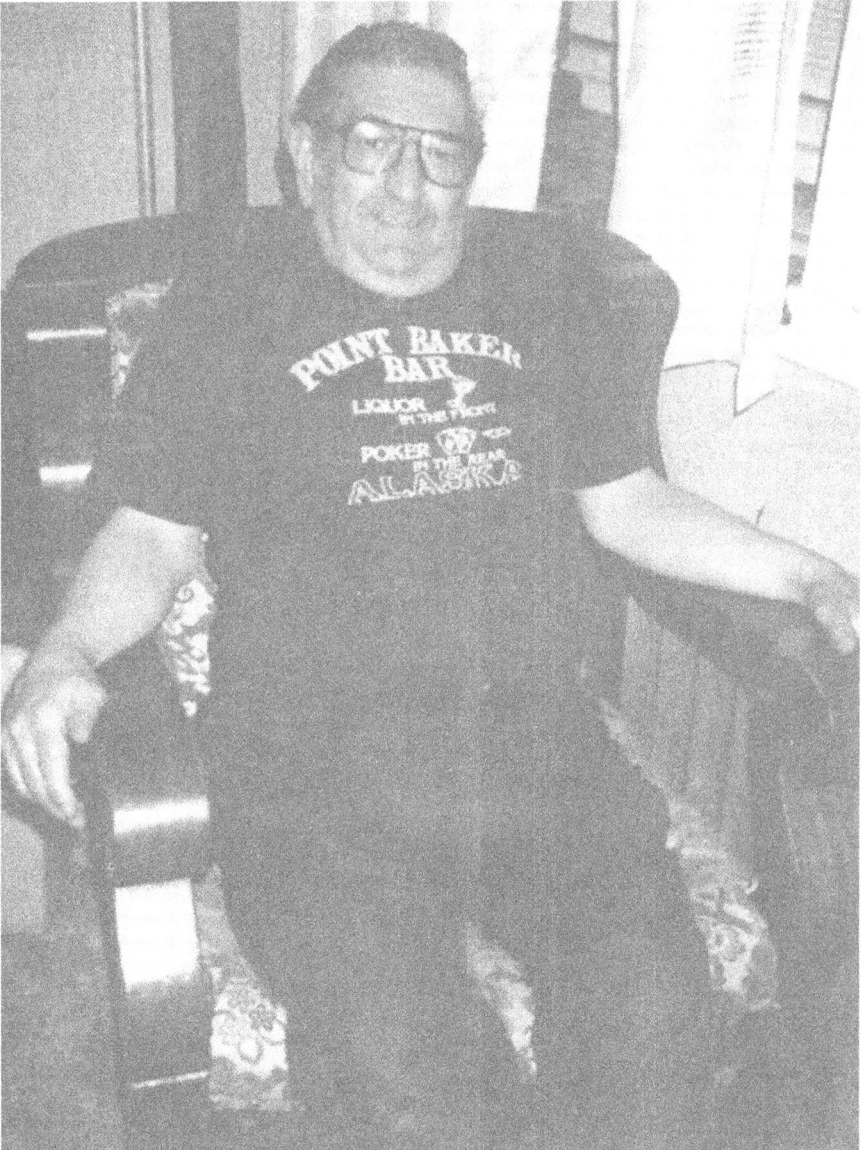

While in the process of moving out of the Stone House in May 29, 1996, he takes a pause in George Titlow's old rocking chair.

Carl & Fannie Ross
Easter 1998

Carl Ross supervises as Terry Wise (backing into the door) and Tom Kadar move Fannie & himself into their new home in Hopwood. May 1996. Young Terry Wise (Junior) also supervises to the right. Bottom photo shows the front of their home.

The Stone House Restaurant & Hotel 1996-1998

Fannie Ross' health let her down. She had wanted to live out her life in the Stone House. At the age of 87, she decided not to re-open. Neither she nor son, Carl, could do it anymore. Millie and her waitress friend Joan, begged Fannie to let them open, but she knew it was time to pass the torch.

On August 7, 1996 Fred and Rhonda Zeigler bought the Stone House and 37.957 acres from Fenalba Ross for $260,000.00. They immediately began remodeling. Today three floors of inn rooms glisten with antiques. Fireplaces gleam throughout dining and hotel rooms, hard wood floors shine, and Millie continues to serve up her dining room humor.

The Stone House is listed on the National Register of Historic Buildings. It's food also goes down in history. When Zeigler bought the Stone House, he knew that following in Fannie's footsteps would not be easy. She was famous for her Italian cuisine and he meant to make her proud.

Stone House Executive Chef Carl Fazio was named "Chef of the Year" in January 1996 by the Pittsburgh Chapter of the American Culinary Association. His creative menu brings diners back for more Artichoke Dip with Crabmeat Brushetta, Seafood Celena Marie, and General Marshall's Chicken & Dumplings.

Fazio is a true specialist in the art of fine cuisine. He was one of the chefs who prepared the Second Inaugural Dinner for President Reagan following his apprenticeship at Hyehold Restaurant in Coraopolis. Here he advanced the establishment to a four star rating. After serving as Chef at Nemacolin Woodlands in Farmington (Pennsylvania's only four star resort), he worked as Executive Chef at Fox Chapel Country Club in Pittsburgh.

"Chef Carl" has won silver and bronze medals in culinary competitions and knows that consistency is the key to a successful operation. Monday mornings he entertains listeners on Uniontown's WMBS Radio Station with his cooking tips. With Fazio's culinary expertise, the Zeiglers have indeed made Fannie proud.

Plans are on the table to expand the tavern, construct new restrooms, and to add a banquet hall matching the original building. Hold your special event at the historical Stone House.

Today's Stone House. Top photo shows the new wall protecting Stone House customer vehichles from Route 40 traffic. George Titlow had a wall built in this fashion to help seclude their swimming pool. The pool is gone now. When Fannie bought the place she had 40 truckloads of dirt hauled out of it, but it kept filling up from the hillside. Bottom photo shows front of building.

In 1996, when her parents first bought the Stone House, Jordon Zeigler played with Fannie's old cash register in the center dining room. At this time the place was closed (except the tavern) and this room was filled with tables and miscellaneous furniture. We can all remember Fannie sitting in the front lobby at this cash register. She just pushed "No Sale" and made change. No computers for her!

The upstairs sitting room where folks staying at the inn can relax, enjoy the morning sun, and soak up the ambiance that is the Stone House.

The Titlow Room is on the 2nd floor. This was George Titlow's bedroom. It has a private bathroom and the most comfortable bed a human could ever experience.

Jim Hasley's construction crew remodels the frame house next to the Stone House. This is where Terry Wise grew up.

Top photo: The old tavern This is scheduled to be remodeled and extended this year. Bottom photo: Jim Hasley supervises as John Leer and helper repair one of the fireplaces in the center dining room.

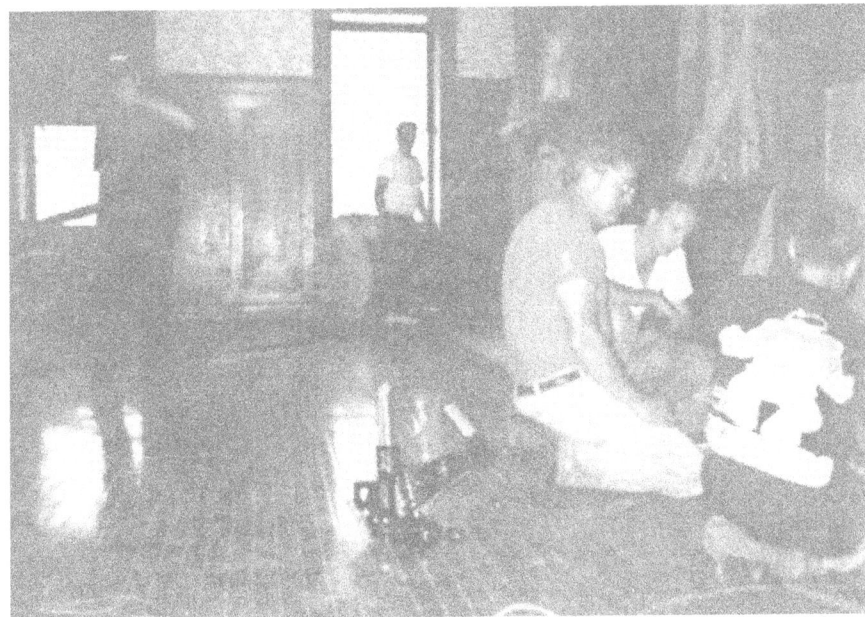

Debbie and Mike Konechny enjoy bananas and carmalized oranges over cappucino ice cream at the WMBS 1997 60th anniversary celebration live at the Stone House.

Banana & Carmalized Oranges
(Serves six)

1 1/2 pints vanilla ice cream
4 small firm but ripe bananas
1 sliced & seeded orange
1T. margarine
2T. light brown sugar
1/4t. cinnamon

Melt margarine, dissolve brown sugar in that. Add fruit, stirring quickly in thin copper skillet. Add cinnamon. Serve over ice cream.

The non smoking dining room to your right when you walk in the front entrance. This room has two fire places and a wonderful archway which allows diners a view of the lobby. A very light and airy room.

This archway takes you to the non smoking dining room to the llobby. The stairs leading from the lobby to the inn rooms is shown with vintage photographs running up the wall along the way.

Cheryl Brozick works the Stone House booth at the annual Rib Festival held at Linden Hall in the summer of 1997.She is serving brushetta. Billy Price and the Keystone Band entertained guests who not only ate ribs all day, but enjoyed a classic car show.

Franco Harris visits the Stone House in 1997 for a Steeler Bash and Auction.

Robin Fisher and Joel Means greet ex-Steeler Tunch Illkin at the 1997 Steeler Bash. Pam Bendeshaw in background.

Fred and Rhonda Zeigler would like to thank all those who co operated to make this publication a reality including contributors:

Fannie and Carl Ross, Edna and Kenneth Smithburger, Millie Pascanik, Diane Pascanik Gordon, Terry Wise, Mark Miner, Mrs. Lawrence Titlow, and the Yesteryear Museum.

For an historic experience of great taste, visit the Stone House Restaurant & Inn today!

Above is only part of the intregal staff that keeps the Stone House running and in top shape. From left to right: First Row: Nancy McDonald, Millie Pascanik, Tammy Bowlen, Gary Evans, Cheryl Brozik, and Nikki Lewis. Second Row: Robby Turner, Brad George, Pat Hoerter, Executive Chef Carl Fazio, Scott Sucke, Mike Dick, and Lorrie Rittenhouse.

www.ingramcontent.com/pod-product-compliance
Lightning Source LLC
Chambersburg PA
CBHW071820020426
42331CB00007B/1566